# Succeeding with the Masters®
# THE FESTIVAL COLLECTION®

## Compiled and edited by HELEN MARLAIS

## About the Series

Welcome to *The Festival Collection*®! This nine-volume series is designed to give students and teachers a great variety of fabulous repertoire from the Baroque, Classical, Romantic, and Twentieth/Twenty-First Centuries. The series is carefully leveled from elementary through advanced repertoire. These pieces are true crowd pleasers and will showcase students' technical and musical abilities. Each level covers the gamut of your repertoire needs, from works that showcase power and bravura, to pieces that develop a student's sense of control and finesse. Having a wide selection of works with pedagogically-correct leveling will help make your repertoire selections easier and your students' performances more successful.

Each book has free downloadable recordings of all of the corresponding works to guide students in their interpretation. The editing in the scores reflects these recorded performances. While the recorded performances are consistent with the editing in the books, and vice versa, they also demonstrate an appropriate degree of interpretive license. My goal is to instill an appreciation for accurate performances, while nurturing a sense for stylistically appropriate interpretive license. Books one through six were recorded by Helen Marlais, and books seven and eight were recorded by Helen Marlais, Chiu-Ling Lin, and Frances Renzi, giving students at these higher levels the opportunity to hear three different performance styles.

*The Festival Collection*® is a companion series to the *Succeeding with the Masters*® series. *Succeeding with the Masters*® provides the student with practice strategies and valuable information about the musical characteristics of each era. *The Festival Collection*® expands the repertoire selection with numerous additional top-drawer pedagogical works in a wide array of styles, and with different musical and technical demands. There is no duplication of repertoire between these two series. All of the pieces in both series are motivational and exciting for students to learn as well as for teachers to teach!

Enjoy the series!

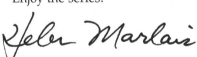

THE
F·J·H
MUSIC
COMPANY
INC.
Frank J. Hackinson

Production: Frank J. Hackinson
Production Coordinator: Philip Groeber
Cover Design and Art Direction: Gwen Terpstra, Terpstra Design, San Francisco, CA, in collaboration with Helen Marlais
Illustration: Keith Criss, TradigitalWorks, Oakland, CA
Engraving: Tempo Music Press, Inc.
Printer: Tempo Music Press, Inc.

ISBN-13: 978-1-56939-594-3

# The Festival Collection® Book 6

| Era | Composer | Title | Page | Track |
|---|---|---|---|---|
| **BAROQUE** | | | | |
| BAROQUE | Bach, Carl Philipp Emanuel | Solfeggietto (*Wq. 117/2*) | 6 | 1 |
| BAROQUE | Scarlatti, Domenico | Sonata in D minor (*K. 89c, L. 211*) | 8 | 2 |
| BAROQUE | Bach, Johann Sebastian | Invention No. 1 in C major (*BWV 772*) | 12 | 3 |
| BAROQUE | Bach, Johann Sebastian | Invention No. 8 in F major (*BWV 779*) | 14 | 4 |
| BAROQUE | Bach, Johann Sebastian | Invention No. 13 in A minor (*BWV 784*) | 16 | 5 |
| BAROQUE | Leo, Leonardo | Toccata in G minor | 18 | 6 |
| BAROQUE | Pergolesi, Giovanni Battista | Allegro | 20 | 7 |
| BAROQUE | Seixas, Carlos de | Toccata in F minor | 23 | 8 |
| BAROQUE | Couperin, François | The Grape Pickers | 26 | 9 |
| BAROQUE | Wagenseil, Georg Christoph | Divertimento | 28 | 10 |
| **CLASSICAL** | | | | |
| CLASSICAL | Cimarosa, Domenico | Sonata No. 18 in A major | 30 | 11 |
| CLASSICAL | Haydn, Franz Joseph | Sonata in G major (*Hob. XVI/27, Movement 3*) | 33 | 12 |
| CLASSICAL | Beethoven, Ludwig van | Sonatina in E flat major (*WoO 47, No. 1, Movement 1*) | 38 | 13 |
| CLASSICAL | Kuhlau, Friedrich | Sonatina in C major (*Op. 55, No. 3, Movement 1*) | 42 | 14 |
| CLASSICAL | Voříšek, Jan Václav | Rondo (*Op. 18*) | 46 | 15 |
| CLASSICAL | Kuhlau, Friedrich | Sonatina in C major (*Op. 88, No. 1*) | 50 | 16, 17, 18 |
| CLASSICAL | Mozart, Wolfgang Amadeus | Sonata in C major (*K. 545, Movements 2 & 3*) | 57 | 19, 20 |
| CLASSICAL | Pleyel, Ignace Joseph | Rondo Grazioso | 64 | 21 |

| Era | Composer | Title | Page | Track |
|-----|----------|-------|------|-------|
| **ROMANTIC** | | | | |
| ROMANTIC | Grieg, Edvard | Cradle Song (*Op. 68, No. 5*) | 66 | 22 |
| ROMANTIC | Chopin, Frédéric | Prelude in E minor (*Op. 28, No. 4*) | 68 | 23 |
| ROMANTIC | Schumann, Robert | From Foreign Lands and People (*Op. 15, No. 1*) | 69 | 24 |
| ROMANTIC | Liadov, Anatol | Prelude (*Op. 40, No. 3*) | 70 | 25 |
| ROMANTIC | Burgmüller, Johann Friedrich | Morning Bell (*Op. 109, No. 9*) | 72 | 26 |
| ROMANTIC | Kalinnikov, Vasili | Chanson triste | 74 | 27 |
| ROMANTIC | Schumann, Robert | Fantasy Dance (*Op. 124, No. 5*) | 76 | 28 |
| ROMANTIC | Chopin, Frédéric | Mazurka in B flat major (*Op. 7, No. 1*) | 78 | 29 |
| ROMANTIC | Franck, César | Sketch | 80 | 30 |
| ROMANTIC | Burgmüller, Johann Friedrich | The Storm (*L'Orage, Op. 109, No. 13*) | 82 | 31 |
| ROMANTIC | Grieg, Edvard | Little Troll (*Op. 71, No. 3*) | 84 | 32 |
| ROMANTIC | Chopin, Frédéric | Valse in A minor (*KK IVb, No. 11*) | 87 | 33 |
| **20TH/21ST CENTURIES** | | | | |
| 20TH/21ST CENT | Kabalevsky, Dmitri | Rondo Toccata (*Op. 60, No. 4*) | 90 | 34 |
| 20TH/21ST CENT | Villa-Lobos, Heitor | No fundo do meu quintal (*Deep in My Backyard*) | 94 | 35 |
| 20TH/21ST CENT | Torjussen, Trygve | To the Rising Sun (*Op. 4, No. 1*) | 96 | 36 |
| 20TH/21ST CENT | Bartók, Béla | Joc cu bâtă (*Stick Dance*) | 98 | 37 |
| 20TH/21ST CENT | Ninov, Dimitar | Golden Leaves | 100 | 38 |
| 20TH/21ST CENT | Martinů, Bohuslav | On the Farm | 102 | 39 |
| 20TH/21ST CENT | Pinto, Octavio | Run, Run! | 105 | 40 |
| 20TH/21ST CENT | Janáček, Leoš | A Blown-Away Leaf (from *On An Overgrown Path*) | 108 | 41 |
| 20TH/21ST CENT | Diemer, Emma Lou | Busy Toccata | 110 | 42 |
| 20TH/21ST CENT | Tansman, Alexandre | Moment sérieux | 113 | 43 |
| 20TH/21ST CENT | Schmitt, Florent | Petit Musique (*Op. 33, No. 8*) | 114 | 44 |
| **ABOUT THE PIECES AND COMPOSERS** | | | 116-124 | |

FJH1590

# The Festival Collection® Book 6

| Composer | Title | Theme | Page | Track |
|---|---|---|---|---|
| Bach, Carl Philipp Emanuel | Solfeggietto (Wq. 117/2) | | 6 | 1 |
| Bach, Johann Sebastian | Invention No. 1 in C major (BWV 772) | | 12 | 3 |
| Bach, Johann Sebastian | Invention No. 8 in F major (BWV 779) | | 14 | 5 |
| Bach, Johann Sebastian | Invention No. 13 in A minor (BWV 784) | | 16 | 4 |
| Bartók, Béla, | Joc cu bâtă (Stick Dance) | | 98 | 37 |
| Beethoven, Ludwig van | Sonatina in E flat major (WoO 47, No. 1, Movement 1) | | 38 | 13 |
| Burgmüller, Johann Friedrich | Morning Bell (Op. 109, No. 9) | | 72 | 26 |
| Burgmüller, Johann Friedrich | The Storm (L'Orage, Op. 109, No. 13) | | 82 | 31 |
| Chopin, Frédéric | Mazurka in B flat major (Op. 7, No. 1) | | 78 | 29 |
| Chopin, Frédéric | Prelude in E minor (Op. 28, No. 4) | | 68 | 23 |
| Chopin, Frédéric | Valse in A minor (KK IVb, No. 11) | | 87 | 33 |
| Cimarosa, Domenico | Sonata No. 18 in A major | | 30 | 11 |
| Couperin, François | The Grape Pickers | | 26 | 9 |
| Diemer, Emma Lou | Busy Toccata | | 110 | 42 |
| Franck, César | Sketch | | 80 | 30 |
| Grieg, Edvard | Cradle Song (Op. 68, No. 5) | | 66 | 22 |
| Grieg, Edvard | Little Troll (Op. 71, No. 3) | | 84 | 32 |
| Haydn, Franz Joseph | Sonata in G major (Hob. XVI/27, Movement 3) | | 33 | 12 |
| Janáček, Leoš | A Blown-Away Leaf (from On An Overgrown Path) | | 108 | 41 |
| Kabalevsky, Dmitri | Rondo Toccata (Op. 60, No. 4) | | 90 | 34 |

Kalinnikov, Vasili . . . . . . . . . . . . . Chanson triste . . . . . . . . . . . . . . . . 74 . . . . . 27

Kuhlau, Friedrich . . . . . . . . . . . . . Sonatina in C major . . . . . . . . . . . . 42 . . . . . 14
*(Op. 55, No. 3, Movement 1)*

Kuhlau, Friedrich . . . . . . . . . . . . . Sonatina in C major . . . . . . . . . . . . 50 . . . . . 16, 17, 18
*(Op. 88, No. 1)*

Leo, Leonardo . . . . . . . . . . . . . . . Toccata in G minor . . . . . . . . . . . . . 18 . . . . . 6

Liadov, Anatol . . . . . . . . . . . . . . . Prelude *(Op. 40, No. 3)* . . . . . . . . . . 70 . . . . . 25

Martinů, Bohuslav . . . . . . . . . . . . On the Farm . . . . . . . . . . . . . . . . . 102 . . . . 39

Mozart, Wolfgang Amadeus . . . . . Sonata in C major . . . . . . . . . . . . . 57 . . . . 19, 20
*(K. 545, Movements 2 & 3)*

Ninov, Dimitar . . . . . . . . . . . . . . . Golden Leaves . . . . . . . . . . . . . . . . 100 . . . . 38

Pergolesi, Giovanni Battista . . . . . . Allegro . . . . . . . . . . . . . . . . . . . . . 20 . . . . . 7

Pinto, Octavio . . . . . . . . . . . . . . . Run, Run! . . . . . . . . . . . . . . . . . . . 105 . . . . 40

Pleyel, Ignace Joseph . . . . . . . . . . Rondo Grazioso . . . . . . . . . . . . . . . 64 . . . . . 21

Scarlatti, Domenico . . . . . . . . . . . . Sonata in D minor . . . . . . . . . . . . . 8 . . . . . 2
*(K. 89c, L. 211)*

Schmitt, Florent . . . . . . . . . . . . . . Petit Musique *(Op. 33, No. 8)* . . . . . . 114 . . . . 44

Schumann, Robert . . . . . . . . . . . . Fantasy Dance *(Op. 124, No. 5)* . . . 76 . . . . . 28

Schumann, Robert . . . . . . . . . . . . From Foreign Lands and People . . 69 . . . . . 24
*(Op. 15, No. 1)*

Seixas, Carlos de . . . . . . . . . . . . . Toccata in F minor . . . . . . . . . . . . . 23 . . . . . 8

Tansman, Alexandre . . . . . . . . . . . Moment sérieux . . . . . . . . . . . . . . . 113 . . . . 43

Torjussen, Trygve . . . . . . . . . . . . . To the Rising Sun *(Op. 4, No. 1)* . . . 96 . . . . 36

Villa-Lobos, Heitor . . . . . . . . . . . . No fundo do meu quintal . . . . . . . 94 . . . . 35
*(Deep in My Backyard)*

Voříšek, Jan Václav . . . . . . . . . . . . Rondo *(Op. 18)* . . . . . . . . . . . . . . . 46 . . . . . 15

Wagenseil, Georg Christoph . . . . . Divertimento . . . . . . . . . . . . . . . . . 28 . . . . . . 10

# SOLFEGGIETTO

*(Wq. 117/2)*

Carl Philipp Emanuel Bach
(1714-1788)

(a) Optional: (b) Later sources end:

N.B. The notes in parentheses are not included in the earliest source.

# SONATA

*(K. 89c, L. 211)*

Domenico Scarlatti
(1685-1757)

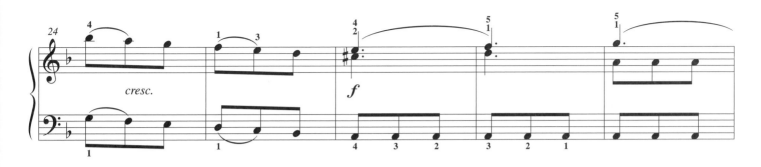

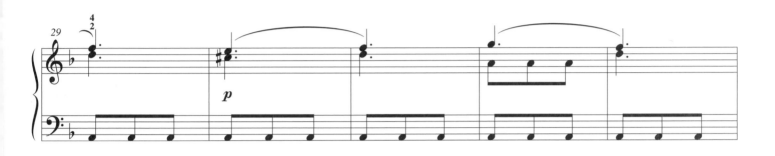

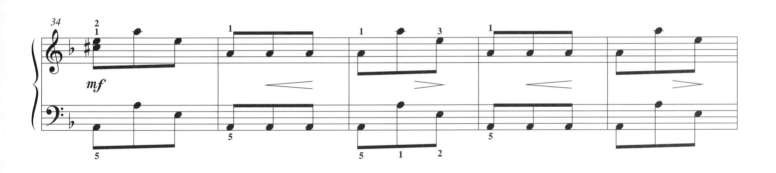

(a)

*original:

(a) Optional trill: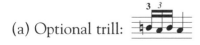

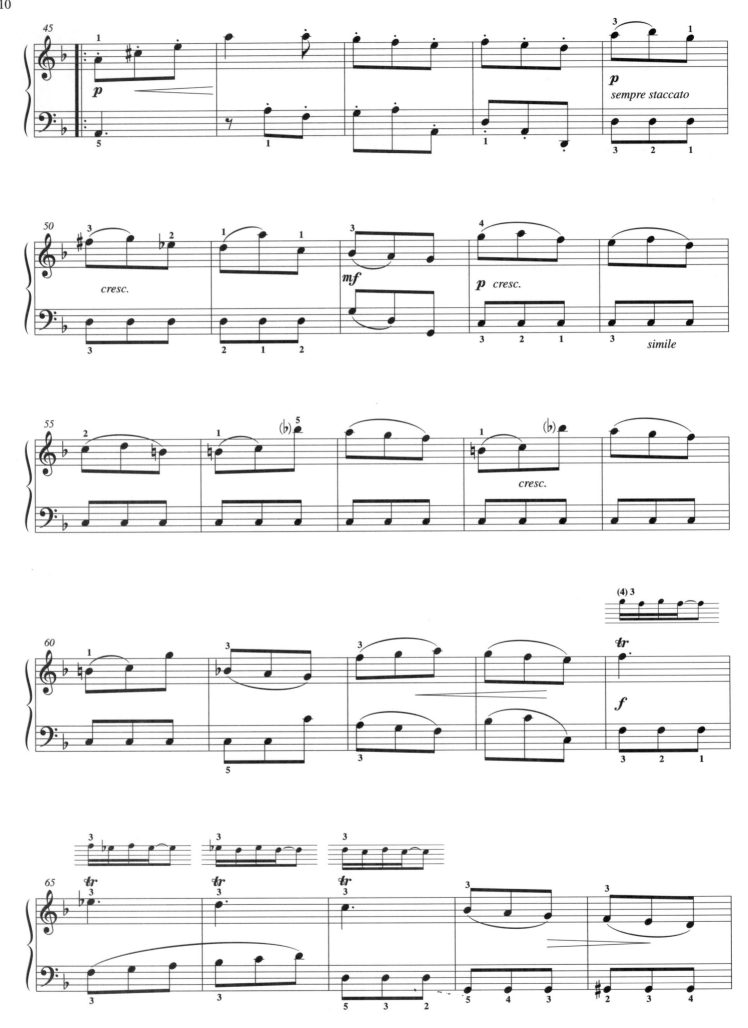

*original:

# INVENTION NO. 1

## *(BWV 772)*

Johann Sebastian Bach
(1685-1750)

# INVENTION NO. 8

## (*BWV 779*)

Johann Sebastian Bach
(1685-1750)

*N.B.* All eighth notes should be played slightly detached.

# INVENTION No. 13

## (BWV 784)

Johann Sebastian Bach
(1685-1750)

# TOCCATA IN G MINOR

Leonardo Leo
(1694-1744)

**Moderato** (♩. = ca. 63)
*sempre legato*

*N.B.* All eighth notes should be played slightly detached unless otherwise noted.

# ALLEGRO

from *Harpsichord Suite No. 1*

Giovanni Battista Pergolesi
(1710-1736)

*N.B.* All eighth notes should be played slightly detached unless otherwise noted.

21

FJH1590

# TOCCATA IN F MINOR

Carlos de Seixas
(1704-1742)

FJH1590

# THE GRAPE PICKERS

*(Les Vendangeuses)*

François Couperin
(1668-1733)

# DIVERTIMENTO

Georg Christoph Wagenseil
(1715-1777)

**Ricercata** (♩ = ca. 152)

*N.B.* The notes in parentheses are not included in the earliest source.

# SONATA NO. 18

Domenico Cimarosa
(1749-1801)

N.B. The Italian term *spigliato* means "to play with freedom."

# SONATA

*(Hob. XVI/27, Third Movement: Finale)*

Franz Joseph Haydn
(1732-1809)

(a) Optional ornament:

(b) Optional ornament:

*dedicated to the Elector Archbishop of Cologne, Maximilian Friedrich*

# SONATINA

*(WoO 47, No. 1, First Movement)*

Ludwig van Beethoven
(1770-1827)

**Allegro cantabile (♩ = 112)**

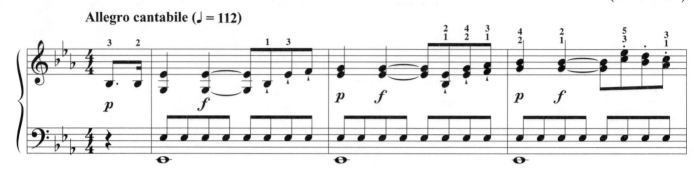

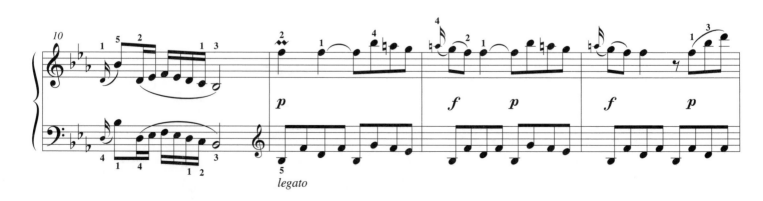

# SONATINA

*(Opus 55, No. 3, First Movement)*

Friedrich Kuhlau
(1786-1832)

**Allegro con spirito (♩ = 116-126)**

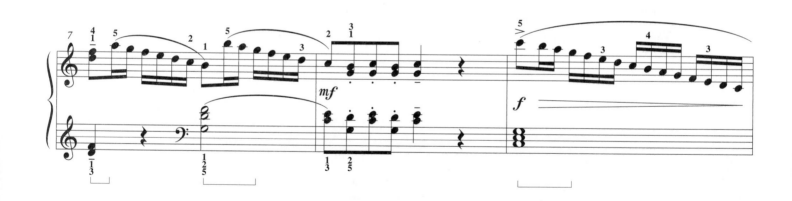

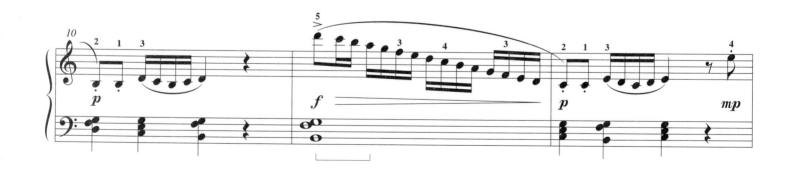

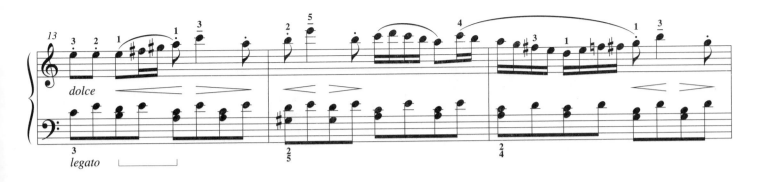

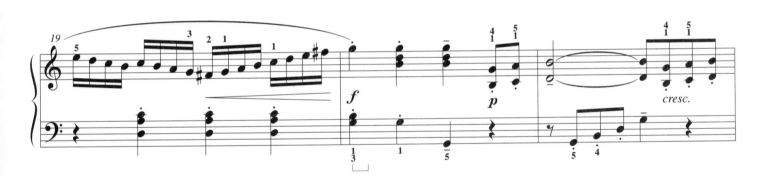

44

# RONDO
## *(Opus 18)*

Jan Václav Voříšek
(1791-1825)

# SONATINA
## *(Opus 88, No. 1)*

Friedrich Kuhlau
(1786-1832)

**RONDO**
Allegro (♩ = 112)

# SONATA

*(K. 545, Second and Third Movements)*

Wolfgang Amadeus Mozart
(1756-1791)

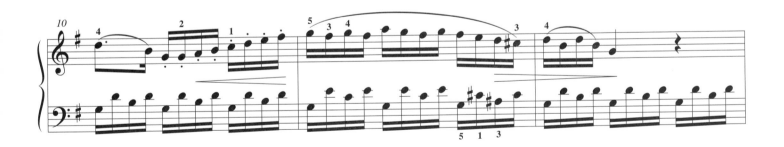

FJH1590

58

FJH1590

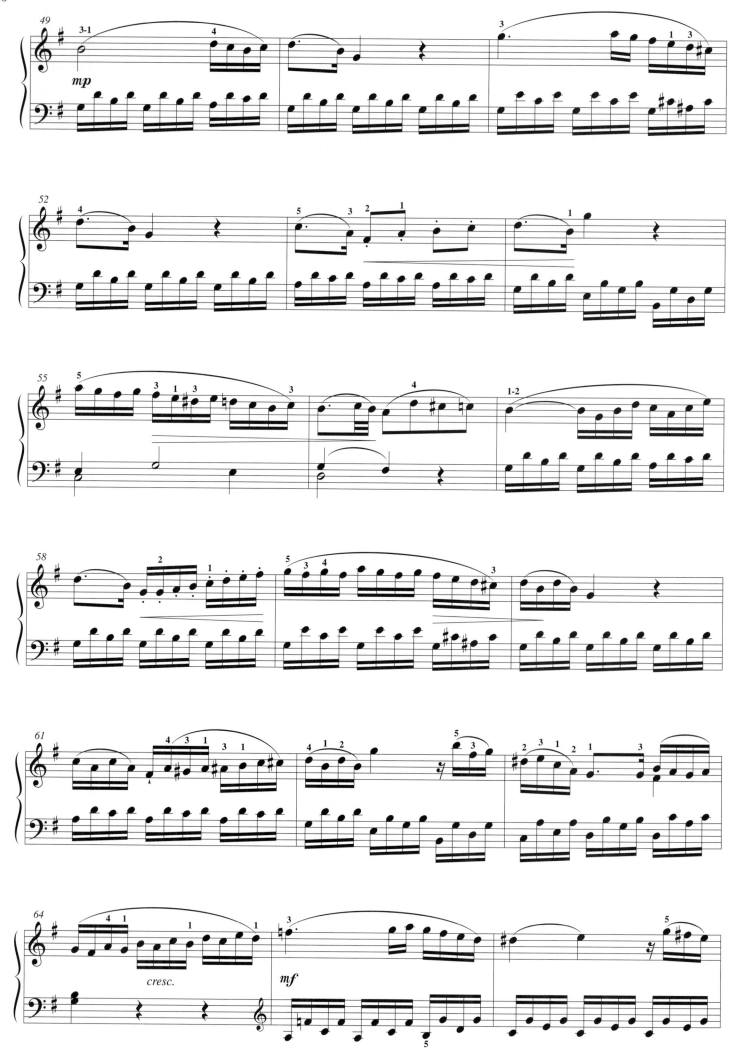

Allegretto (♩ = ca. 88)

# Rondo Grazioso

Ignace Joseph Pleyel
(1757-1831)

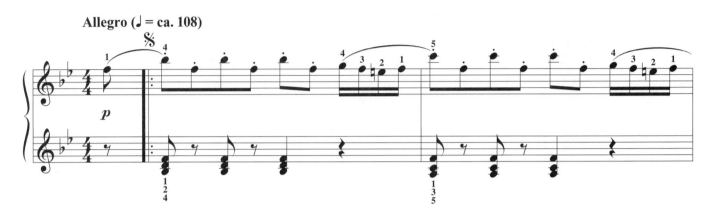

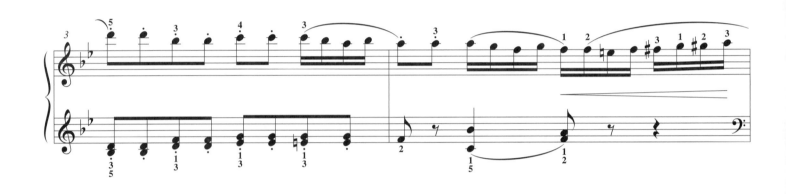

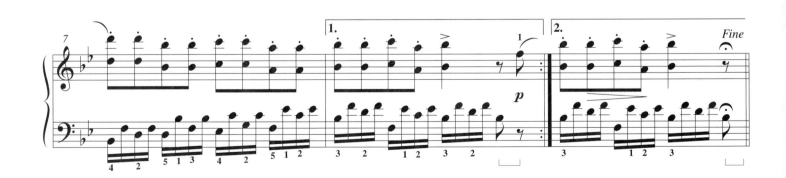

# CRADLE SONG

from *Lyric Pieces, Opus 68, No. 5*

Edvard Grieg
(1843-1907)

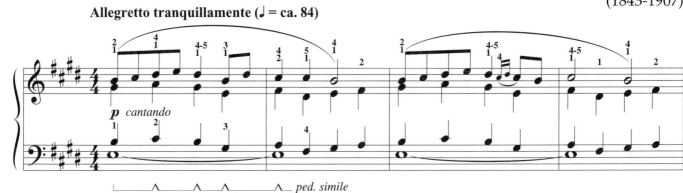

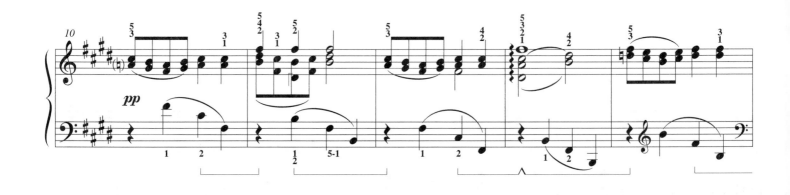

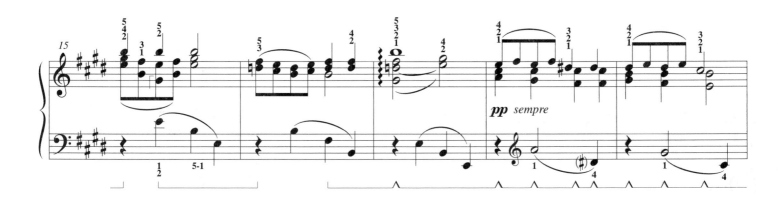

# PRELUDE

## (Opus 28, No. 4)

Frédéric Chopin
(1810-1849)

*N.B.* The pedal markings in measures 17 and 18 are Chopin's.

# FROM FOREIGN LANDS AND PEOPLE

from *Scenes from Childhood, Opus 15, No. 1*

Robert Schumann
(1810-1856)

# PRELUDE
## *(Opus 40, No. 3)*

Anatol Konstantinovich Liadov
(1855-1914)

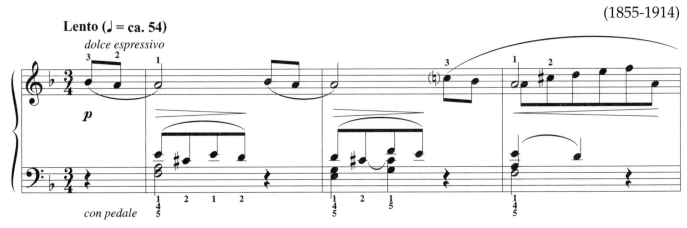

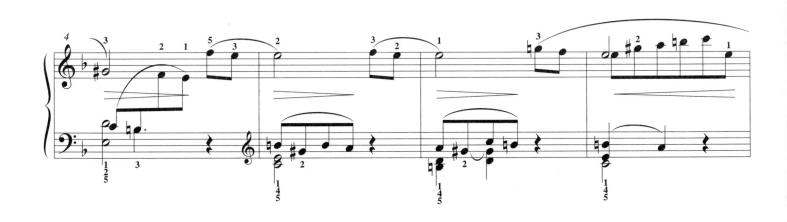

# MORNING BELL

### from *18 Characteristic Studies, Opus 109, No. 9*

Johann  Friedrich Burgmüller
(1806-1874)

**Andante sostenuto** (♩ = 80-88)

# CHANSON TRISTE
## (A Sad Song)

Vasili Sergeyevich Kalinnikov
(1866-1901)

# FANTASY DANCE
## (Opus 124, No. 5)

Robert Schumann
(1810-1856)

Sehr rasch (Very fast) (♩ = ca. 176)

*dedicated to Mr. Johns*

# Mazurka

*(Opus 7, No. 1)*

Frédéric Chopin
(1810-1849)

* Start the trill on the principal note.

# SKETCH

César Franck
(1822-1890)

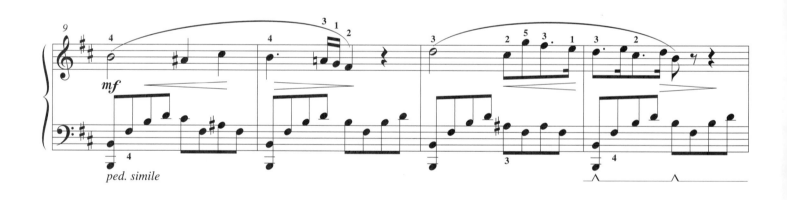

# THE STORM

*L'Orage,* from *18 Characteristic Studies,*
*Opus 109, No. 13*

Johann Friedrich Burgmüller
(1806-1874)

# LITTLE TROLL

*Puck,* from *Lyric Pieces, Opus 71, No. 3*

Edvard Grieg
(1843-1907)

**Allegro molto** (♩ = 138)

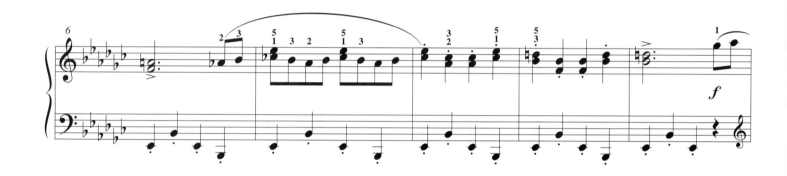

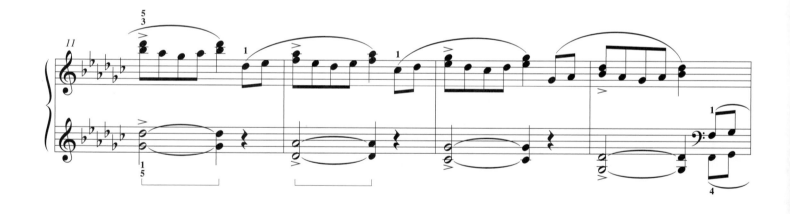

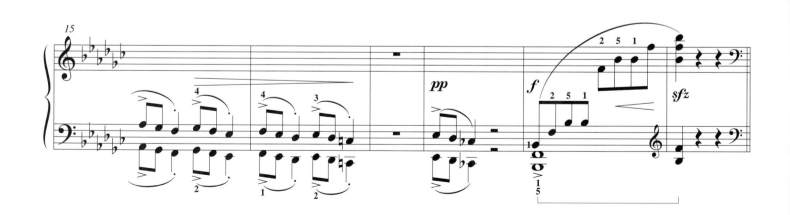

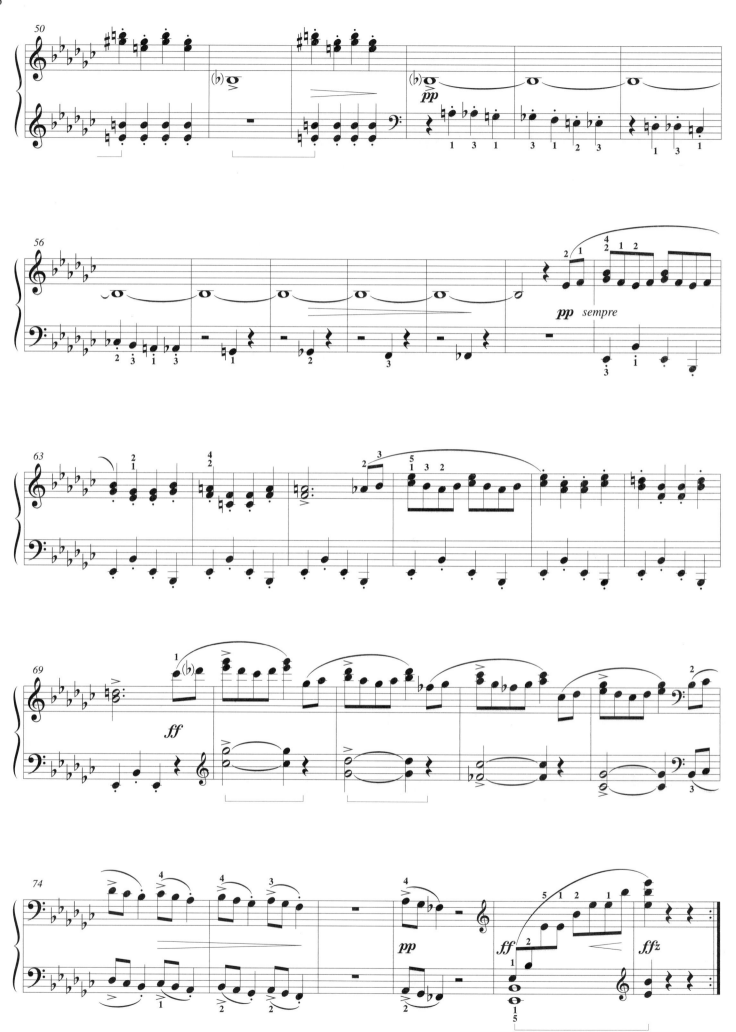

# VALSE

*(Waltz, KK IVb, No. 11)*

Frédéric Chopin
(1810-1849)

**Allegretto** (♩ = 104-112)

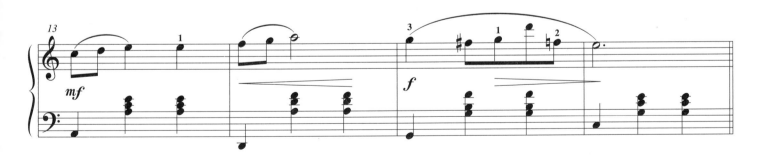

# RONDO TOCCATA

from *Four Rondos for Piano, Opus 60, No. 4*

Dmitri Borisovich Kabalevsky
(1904-1987)

**Allegro scherzando** (♩ = ca. 176)

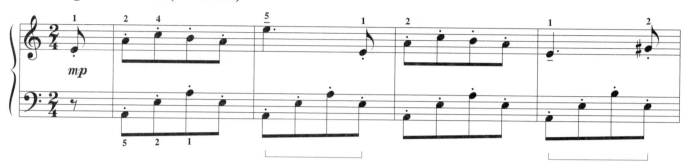

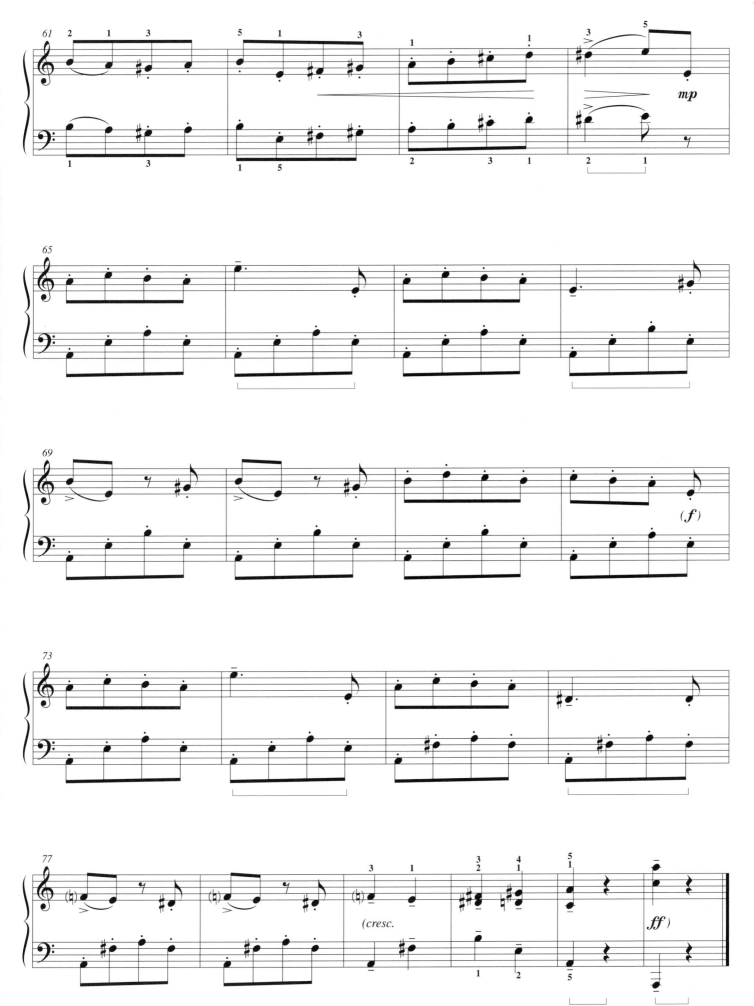

# No fundo do meu quintal

*Deep in My Backyard* from *Twice Five Pieces*, from *Guia Pratico for Piano*

Heitor Villa-Lobos
(1887-1959)

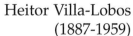

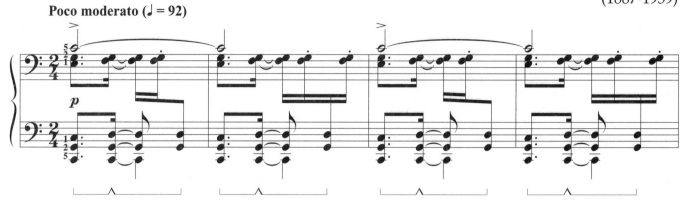

# TO THE RISING SUN

## (Opus 4, No. 1)

Trygve Torjussen
(1885-1977)

# Joc cu Bâtă

*Stick Dance* from *Romanian Folk Dances, Sz. 56*

Béla Bartók
(1881-1945)

N.B. The tempo, articulation, and pedal markings are Bartok's. *Sopra* and *sotto* means to play the R.H. *over* the L.H.

# GOLDEN LEAVES

from *Piano Album*

Dimitar Ninov
(1963-    )

**Doloroso e cantabile** (♩. = 54)

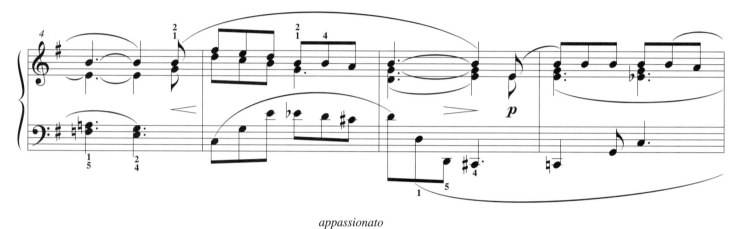

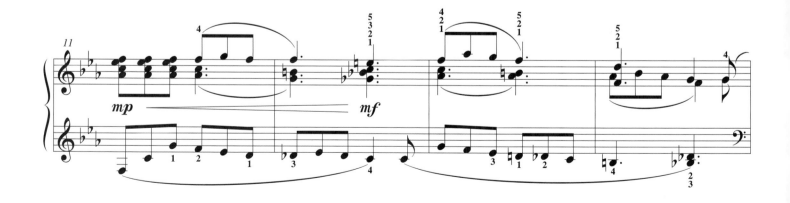

FJH1590

# ON THE FARM

*Na farmě* from *Fables, H. 138*

Bohuslav Martinů
(1890-1959)

# RUN, RUN!
## from *Memories of Childhood*

Octavio Pinto
(1890-1950)

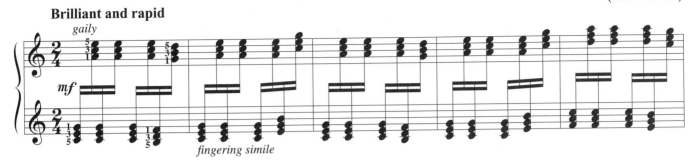

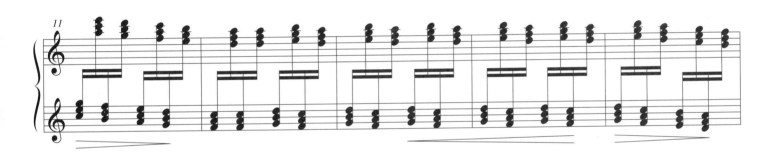

FJH1590

The Organ-Grinder passes by

con pedale

fading away

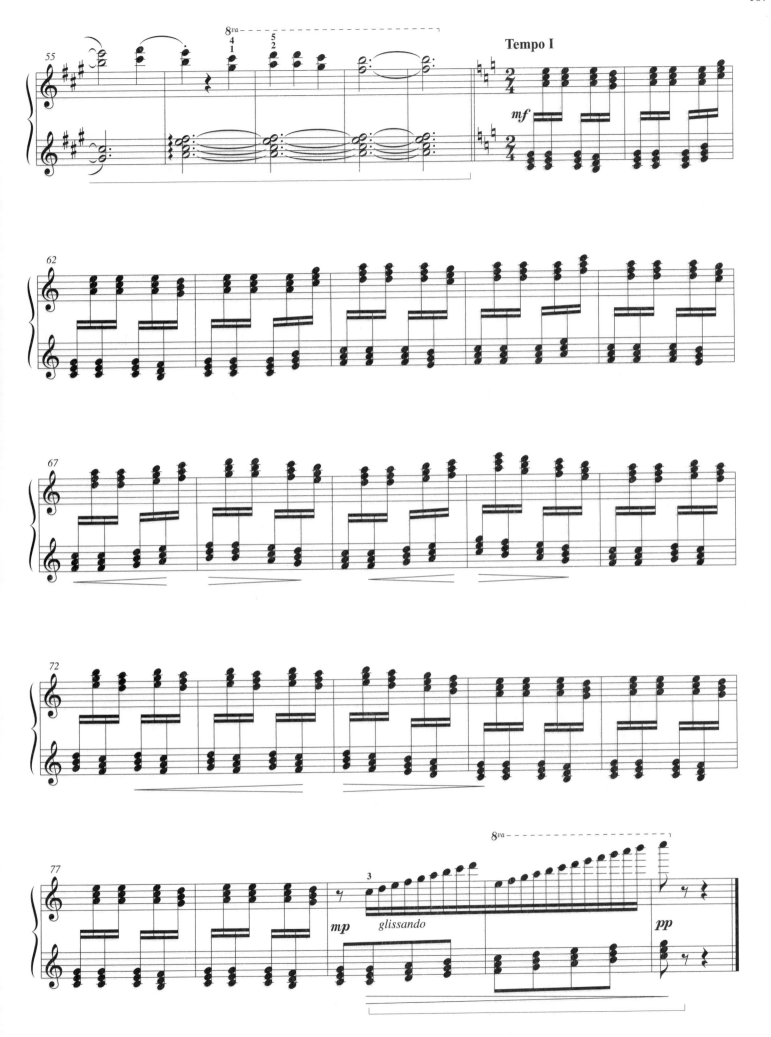

# A Blown-Away Leaf

from *On An Overgrown Path*

Leoš Janáček
(1854-1928)

# BUSY TOCCATA

from *Reaching Out, for Solo Piano*

Emma Lou Diemer
(1927-     )

**As fast as possible (♩ = 120)**

*Very detached all the way through*

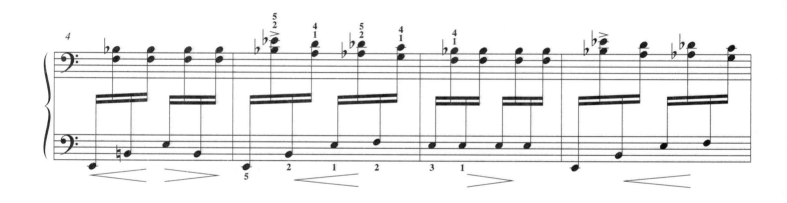

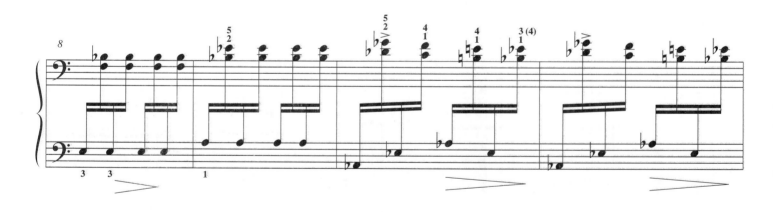

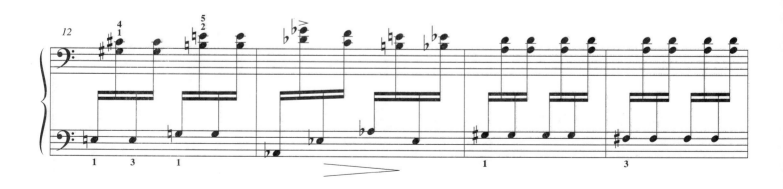

# Moment sérieux

*A Serious Moment,* from *Pour les Enfants, Vol. 4*

Alexandre Tansman
(1897-1986)

# Petit Musique
## (Opus 33, No. 8)

Florent Schmitt
(1870-1958)

# ABOUT THE PIECES AND THE COMPOSERS

## BAROQUE ERA

**Solfeggietto** (Wq. 117/2), by Carl Philipp Emanuel Bach (1714-1788)
Carl Philipp Emanuel (C.P.E.) Bach was the third and most illustrious of Johann Sebastian Bach's sons. He started to compose keyboard pieces when he was sixteen years old and continued to write them until the last years of his life—marches, minuets, and polonaises. He developed the sonata form, and wrote the *Essay on the True Art of Playing Keyboard Instruments* that was used by generations of musicians. Mozart was his contemporary, and highly regarded the music of C.P.E. Bach. A *solfeggio* is a sight-reading or vocal exercise in which the Italian syllables *do, re, mi, fa, sol, la, ti,* and *do* are used for the notes in the scale. This particular edition of the *Solfeggietto* is taken from the first edition of 1770.

**Sonata in D minor** (K. 89c, L. 211), by Domenico Scarlatti (1685-1757)
This Italian musician's influence is lasting. At the age of fifteen he was already an organist and composer. Scarlatti moved to Portugal where he became the harpsichord teacher to the king's daughter Maria Barbara. He took an interest in short forms and over 500 of his attractive, one-movement, binary-form (AB) sonatas were written as *esercizi* (exercises) for her. The *Sonata in D minor* is only one of eight of these sonatas which was composed for violin with figured bass, or *basso continuo,* in which the keyboard player, supported by another instrument, improvises and makes the bass line "continuous." For more information about Domenico Scarlatti, see *Succeeding with the Masters*®, Baroque Era, Volume Two.

**Invention No. 1 in C major** (BWV 772), by Johann Sebastian Bach (1685-1750)
An *invention* is a two- or three-part composition for a keyboard instrument. *Invention* was the term Johann Sebastian Bach chose for the fifteen two-part pieces for keyboard that he composed in 1720 and revised in 1723 (BWV 772-786). They display considerable skill in counterpoint and feature the development of a single theme. The pieces may have evolved from the *ricercare,* an instrumental piece of the sixteenth and seventeenth centuries featuring counterpoint and imitation, a form that reached its culmination in two of Bach's own *ricercares,* composed in Leipzig in 1747 and published in his *Musical Offering.* For more information about J.S. Bach, see *Succeeding with the Masters*®, Baroque Era, Volume Two.

**Invention No. 8 in F major** (BWV 779), by Johann Sebastian Bach (1685-1750)
The Bach family musical dynasty produced musicians from the early sixteenth to the nineteenth centuries. They lived and worked in central Germany, an economically sound and musically sophisticated area. Johann Sebastian Bach was the outstanding figure amongst them. He researched the background of his family and its musical heritage, drawing up a family genealogy. Although the original manuscript of this invention has been lost, several copies still exist, including an important one with additions by C.P.E. Bach.

**Invention No. 13 in A minor** (BWV 784), by Johann Sebastian Bach (1685-1750)
J.S. Bach was a musical genius—a keyboard virtuoso and an extraordinary composer. His performances brought him legendary fame in his lifetime, but his voluminous compositions

have earned him a beloved position in history. He was orphaned at the age of ten and taken in for a time by his older brother. He began composing at an early age and worked professionally as an organist. Bach kept a notebook of keyboard pieces for his wife Anna Magdalena Bach and another notebook of pieces for his eldest son Wilhelm Friedemann. The compositions are played by piano students the world over.

**Toccata in G minor**, by Leonardo Leo (1694-1744)
This important Italian composer studied in Naples, Italy with Nicola Fago. He became the head organist at the chapel there, and later, *primo maestro* at the music conservatory. Versatile and technically skilled, he was one of the leading composers of his day. In addition to sacred music (including vocal), he wrote chamber cantatas, arias and duets, instrumental work, teaching exercises and pieces, and some fifty operas, both comic and serious. *Toccata* is an Italian term for a keyboard composition designed to demonstrate either the performer's ability or the full range and capability of the instrument itself.

**Allegro** (from *Harpsichord Suite No. 1*), by Giovanni Battista Pergolesi (1710-1736)
Although his life was short, this Italian composer became the leading figure in comic opera. He received early musical training on the violin and studied at the Conservatory in Naples, Italy. He composed sacred music (particularly masses), chamber cantatas and duets, *solfeggi* (two- and three-part exercises), as well as instrumental music and serious operas. He was among the most popular and well-respected composers of his generation. His musical style reflected the newly evolving *galant* style, which replaced the seriousness of Baroque music with a lighter, fanciful, witty, coquettish sound.

**Toccata in F minor**, by Carlos de Seixas (1704-1742)
A leading figure in Portuguese music, Seixas was a composer and virtuoso on both the organ and the harpsichord. He held his first post as organist of a cathedral at the age of fourteen. He moved to Lisbon, Portugal and obtained the coveted post of organist at the royal chapel, which he maintained throughout his life. Many of his works reflect a highly demanding keyboard technique, as is exemplified in this particular *toccata*. His legacy lies in a significant number of keyboard sonatas (often designated as *toccatas*), sixty-four of which reside in a private collection.

**The Grape Pickers** (Les Vendangeuses), by François Couperin (1668-1733)
From the late sixteenth to the mid-nineteenth centuries, the French family Couperin was one of the great musical dynasties. François Couperin, the most important musician from this lineage, is known as *le grand* (the great). François was an organist and composed two masses at the age of ten. He composed in the *galant* style, characterized by an interest in short forms with an elegant, light, and graceful feeling. Couperin's complete works include a significant number of compositions for the harpsichord, among them *Les Vendangeuses*, which was published in Paris in 1713.

**Divertimento**, by Georg Christoph Wagenseil (1715-1777)
Wagenseil was born in Vienna to a family who served at the Viennese imperial court. He studied keyboard, counterpoint, and composition, and was a renowned composer to the court from 1739 until his death. Both Mozart and Haydn played his works. He wrote sacred and chamber music, operas, symphonies, keyboard concertos and dance suites, a concerto for cello, and one of the first concertos for alto trombone. A *divertimento* (amusement) is an orchestral piece consisting of several short movements. Wagenseil's early works are in the baroque style, as is evident in this piece.

# CLASSICAL ERA

**Sonata No. 18 in A major**, by Domenico Cimarosa (1749-1801)

The Italian composer Cimarosa was a central figure in opera in the late eighteenth century. He studied for eleven years at the Conservatory in Naples, Italy, becoming a fine violinist and keyboard player. He was also a gifted singer. As a student he composed sacred motets and masses, but with the success of his first musical comedy, he continued to compose successful works for the stage. When he held a court appointment in Vienna, his first opera was so successful that Franz Joseph Haydn conducted thirteen performances of his opera at the palace Esterháza. His instrumental works include concertos and many keyboard sonatas. Known for keyboard works and more than sixty operas, he became one of the most popular composers of his day. Rumor has it that poisoning led to his death in Venice.

**Sonata in G major** (Hob. XVI/27, Third Movement: Finale), by Franz Joseph Haydn (1732-1809)

The Baroque sonata was simple, with two sections, each one repeated (binary form). In the Classical era, Haydn was creative in his expansion of the sonata form to include an *exposition,* presenting the thematic material in a movement from the tonic key moving to the dominant; the *development,* transforming the theme into motives and using counterpoint and rapid harmonic changes; and the *recapitulation,* reintroducing the material of the exposition and reasserting the original key. Essential features of the evolving sonata form appear in the works of Haydn, Mozart, and Beethoven. In most classical sonatas, the first movement is in sonata form, the second movement is contrasting in tempo and key, and the third movement often uses a rondo or theme and variation form. The third movement of this particular sonata is a theme and variations, and Haydn playfully changes the theme in a variety of different ways to create a splendid final movement.

**Sonatina in E flat major** (WoO 47, No. 1, First Movement), by Ludwig van Beethoven (1770-1827)

This German composer was the dominant musical figure of the nineteenth century. He transformed every genre in which he worked. At the age of thirty, he fell ill which caused him to lose his hearing, one of the worst fates for a composer. His compositions reflected the classical style in his early years, and as he grew older and went completely deaf, Beethoven composed works that are in the Romantic style, combining classical forms with great depth of personal expression. His music bridged the Classical and Romantic eras. This particular sonatina is a part of *Three Sonatas* (the *Kurfürstensonaten*), composed when Beethoven was only thirteen years old. This work was dedicated to the Elector Archbishop of Cologne, Maximilian Friedrich.

**Sonatina in C major** (Opus 55, No. 3, First Movement), by Friedrich Kuhlau (1786-1832)
This Danish pianist and composer was born in Germany, and was the son of a poor military bandmaster. In 1810 he went to Copenhagen, Denmark, where he became a court chamber musician and chorus master of the Royal Theatre. He traveled widely, and met Beethoven in Vienna in 1825. He became the leading Danish composer of his day, and had a profound influence on Danish music during the nineteenth century. A *sonatina* is a relatively short composition in sonata form, usually written for the piano.

**Rondo** (Opus 18), by Jan Václav Voříšek (1791-1825)
Voříšek was a Bohemian composer, pianist, and organist. He began studying piano and voice when he was only three years old, and later, the organ and violin. He served as an organist for a local church at the young age of seven. From 1813 until his death, he lived in Vienna, Austria. He was among the first to engage in the form of the piano miniature, which is a short piece. He contributed to the development of the *brillante* style of piano music, which contains rapid right-hand sections that require great skill as a pianist. A number of his orchestral works are in *rondo* form, with a primary section or theme and one or more secondary sections.

**Sonatina in C major** (Opus 88, No. 1), by Friedrich Kuhlau (1786-1832)
Kuhlau is best known for his many piano works, which are often used as teaching pieces and include sonatas, sonatinas, rondos, and variations for solo and duet. Although not a flautist himself, he composed many successful compositions for the flute. Kuhlau wrote important vocal music for the stage, including five operas and incidental music to three plays. In his music to *Elverhøf*, which is the most frequently performed play in the Danish repertory, Kuhlau arranged old Danish and Swedish folk tunes to complement the drama.

**Sonata in C major** (K. 545, Second and Third Movements), by Wolfgang Amadeus Mozart (1756-1791)
Although Mozart's short life was marked by a constant struggle for commissions, court appointments, or other sources of income, he made outstanding contributions to almost all musical genres, playing an important role in establishing the Classical style of composition. His sacred music includes eighteen masses and an oratorio. His orchestral works consist of about fifty symphonies, forty concertos (twenty-five of them for piano), and a large quantity of chamber music. Mozart's *Sonata in C major* was composed on June 26, 1788, and published after his death in 1805, under the title *Sonata Facile* (Easy Sonata). However, this piece is deceptively challenging to play! For more information about Mozart, see *Succeeding with the Masters®*, Classical Era, Volume Two.

**Rondo Grazioso**, by Ignace Joseph Pleyel (1757-1831)
Pleyel was born into an Austro-French family of composers, musicians, publishers, and piano manufacturers. As a young man, he studied with Haydn. In 1795 he settled in Paris, France, opening a music shop and a highly successful publishing house. Pleyel organized, composed for, and conducted a series of public concerts. His compositions consisted of orchestral works, chamber music, stage and vocal works, keyboard and harp solos, and Scottish songs that were extremely popular during his lifetime. A *rondo* is a piece with repetitive themes or sections. *Grazioso*, in Italian, means *graceful*.

# ROMANTIC ERA

**Cradle Song** (from *Lyric Pieces*, Opus 68, No. 5), by Edvard Grieg (1843-1907)
Edvard Grieg was Norway's most important composer. He was born in Bergen, Norway, and died there in 1907. He studied at the Leipzig Conservatory in Germany. Rirkard Nordraak, composer of the Norwegian national anthem, was an inspiration to Grieg. More than any other artist before him, Grieg evoked the character of a nation's music. He married the singer Nina Hagerup and performed with her. He was also a conductor and teacher. The piano virtuoso Franz Liszt admired Grieg's famous *Piano Concerto in A minor*. The *Lyric Pieces* are short character pieces for the piano that comprise ten books. These were composed over the years 1867 to 1901. *Cradle Song*, which is a delicate miniature, was written between 1897 and 1899.

**Prelude in E minor** (Opus 28, No. 4), by Frédéric Chopin (1810-1849)
The Polish composer and pianist Frédéric Chopin was born near Warsaw, Poland in 1810, and died at an early age in Paris, France. As a child prodigy, he gained entrée into a small group of wealthy aristocratic families. Chopin's *Preludes Op. 28* were published in 1839. Rather than traditional simple performance pieces, these preludes are works of substance and weight. Each prelude can stand on its own as a gem of the piano repertoire, or they can be performed in groups. The complete preludes are a carefully planned cycle of all the major and minor keys. To play and learn more about the preludes, please see *Succeeding with the Masters*®, Romantic Era, Volume Two.

**From Foreign Lands and People** (from *Scenes from Childhood*, Opus 15, No. 1), by Robert Schumann (1810-1856)
The German pianist and composer Robert Schumann was the son of a bookseller and publisher. He showed musical talent at an early age, and his love of literature contributed to the endearing lyricism of his music. He studied piano with Friedrich Wieck in Vienna (whose daughter Clara became his wife), but an injury to his right hand led him to abandon his hopes of being a performer and instead he turned to composition. Schumann's *Scenes from Childhood (Kinderscenen)* were composed as light piano pieces in 1838. Of this piece, Clara wrote that one can be transported to foreign lands since it is so beautiful. As you play and listen to this piece, does it transport you to another land?

**Prelude** (Opus 40, No. 3), by Anatol Konstantinovich Liadov (Anatoly Lyadov) (1855-1914)
This Russian composer, teacher, and conductor studied piano and violin at the St. Petersburg Conservatory. He was an accomplished pianist and studied compositional techniques such as counterpoint and the fugue. He was an original talent, if somewhat undisciplined, having to be suspended for a time from Rimsky-Korsakov's composition class for failure to attend. He became a teacher of advanced counterpoint and composition, and published arrangements of folksongs he had collected. He wrote three popular and successful orchestral pieces based on Russian fairy tales. His piano miniatures convey Russian drama as well as sensitivity. This *Prelude* was composed in 1897.

**Morning Bell** (from *18 Characteristic Studies*, Opus 109, No. 9),
by Johann Friedrich Burgmüller (1806-1874)
The Burgmüllers were a family of German musicians. Johann Friedrich was born in Regensburg, Germany, as one of two sons of a touring theater conductor and the founder and director of the Lower Rhine Music Festival. Johann's younger brother Norbert was a child prodigy, and although Johann was a more creative composer, he lived much of his life in poverty. He wrote many piano studies and other instructional pieces for children, which are still well-known today. The composer Robert Schumann thought highly of his musical gifts. The important set of piano studies from which this piece is taken is still widely used.

**Chanson triste** *(A Sad Song),* by Vasili Sergeyevich Kalinnikov (1866-1901)
A talented Russian composer and conductor, Kalinnikov played the violin and became director of a seminary choir at the age of fourteen. He studied at the Moscow Philharmonic Music School, and in 1893 was appointed assistant conductor to the Italian Theatre in Moscow. There, he gave private lessons in music theory. Kalinnikov admired the Russian writer Turgenev and, like him, aspired to capture the atmosphere of Russian country life and scenery. Kalinnikov composed dramatic vocal, instrumental, and piano music, including symphonies and incidental music.

**Fantasy Dance** (Opus 124, No. 5), by Robert Schumann (1810-1856)
Robert Schumann enjoyed a loving relationship with his wife and fellow musician, Clara, who was a brilliant pianist. During the early years of their marriage, Robert composed many of his famous songs and song cycles. Clara edited Schumann's compositions, and she was so well-known as a gifted artist that composers would come to ask her advice about their compositions. Robert Schumann is known chiefly for his songs (over 300), and his piano compositions, which included character pieces, variations, and sonatas. He also composed orchestral works, a piano concerto, a cello concerto, chamber music that included three string quartets and three violin sonatas, and several choral works. Schumann created and wrote a great deal for the *New Journal for Music*, and his writings defined him as an expert on music during the era. He promoted new composers with his musical reviews, and discussed music education. The Schumanns became very good friends with another famous composer, Johannes Brahms, who assisted Clara and the children after Robert's death. You can learn more about Schumann in *Succeeding with the Masters*®, Romantic Era, Volume Two.

**Mazurka in B flat major** (Opus 7, No. 1), by Frédéric Chopin (1810-1849)
Born in Poland, Chopin moved to Vienna, Austria in 1830, where he composed his first *mazurkas* (Op. 6 and 7). He then moved to Paris, France, where he remained because of the political instability in Poland. He enjoyed Paris' rich cultural life and the friendship of other young musicians like Franz Liszt and Hector Berlioz. There, he achieved a reputation as an exceptional teacher, as well as a famed performer. Chopin's music takes the pianist to new musical heights of the Romantic piano tradition, where expressiveness and technique are essential. The *mazurka* is a Polish dance.

**Sketch**, by César Franck (1822-1890)
César Franck, one of the leading figures of nineteenth-century French musical life, was born in Belgium. He began musical studies at an early age, and excelled in *solfège* (sight-singing) and piano. When his family moved to Paris, he studied harmony and counterpoint. He became an organist at St. Clotilde, and entered an intensely creative phase that lasted the rest of his life. He developed the *cyclic* form, in which themes are transformed in successive

sections or movements of a piece. Franck was a highly respected and widely influential teacher who was innovative and receptive to his pupils' compositional ideas. *Sketch*, the third piece Franck ever wrote, was written when he was thirteen years old. One of his most impressive, advanced piano works is titled *Prelude, Chorale, and Fugue*.

**The Storm** (*L'Orage*, from *18 Characteristic Studies*, Opus 109, No. 13), by Johann Friedrich Burgmüller (1806-1874)
Burgmüller studied with the German composer and violinist Louis Spohr in Kassel. He settled in Paris in 1832, where he adopted a light style of composition and made his living as a teacher, composer, and pianist. He wrote salon music, songs, and the ballet *La Péri* (The Fairy), which achieved great popularity. His other works include two symphonies, a piano concerto, and other orchestral pieces, as well as piano sonatas and many keyboard miniatures composed in the German Romantic style.

**Little Troll** (*Puck*, from *Lyric Pieces*, Opus 71, No. 3), by Edvard Grieg (1843-1907)
Edvard Grieg wrote over 120 songs based on Norwegian poems. His genius is shown in the composition of lyric pieces—songs and piano miniatures drawn from his love of folk tunes and tradition. Many of Grieg's best-known pieces are contained in the ten sets of *Lyric Pieces* he composed over the years from 1867 to 1901. *Puck* was written in 1901. In addition to the *Lyric Pieces*, which were inspired by Grieg's love for his country, its folklore, and its scenery, Grieg wrote orchestral music, chamber music that included violin sonatas, a cello sonata, and two string quartets, and some large-scale vocal works.

**Valse in A minor** (*Waltz*, KK IVb, No. 11), by Frédéric Chopin (1810-1849)
There were two formal tendencies in Chopin's music: one continuous and directional, the other sectionalized—an expansion of the three-part song form. Chopin was an innovative composer. His music has a unique sound, and his repertoire includes études, scherzos, waltzes, ballades, mazurkas, preludes, fantasias, impromptus, nocturnes, songs, and his nationalistic polonaises. In his final years, Chopin reached an eloquent simplicity in his compositions. Chopin's *Waltz in A minor* was composed in 1847, just two years before his death.

# 20TH/21ST CENTURIES

**Rondo Toccata** (from *Four Rondos for Piano*, Opus 60, No.4), by Dmitri Borisovich Kabalevsky (1904-1987)
This Russian composer's first major work, *Poem of Struggle,* depicts the atmosphere of Russian life. He wrote sonatas, operas, symphonies, a cello sonata, as well as twenty-four preludes for piano based on Russian folksongs. His greatest legacy lies in the field of compositions for children: music for children's choruses, piano music, and a series of concertos for violin, cello, and piano. Several of his instrumental concertos for young musicians gained worldwide popularity. He also developed an important system of music education for children.

**No fundo do meu quintal** (*Deep in My Backyard,* from *Twice Five Pieces*, from *Guia Pratico for Piano*), by Heitor Villa-Lobos (1887-1959)
Villa-Lobos was born in Rio de Janeiro, Brazil. Trained in classical music, the cello was his

favorite instrument. Between 1850 and 1920, while fashionable European dances were popular in Rio, Villa-Lobos was drawn to the strolling musicians known as *chorões* (weepers), singers of a kind of popular Brazilian tune. He traveled throughout Brazil and the Amazon, and between 1920 and 1945 composed the *Chôros*, a sequence of sixteen works communicating the sounds of his country, establishing him as Brazil's foremost nationalistic musical voice. His musical output was enormous, totaling 1000 works. This particular work was written in Rio, in 1935.

**To the Rising Sun** (Opus 4, No. 1), by Trygve Torjussen (1885-1977)
Torjussen was a Norwegian pianist, composer, and teacher, whose career flourished in the early part of the twentieth century. His *Norseland Sketches, Op. 7*, written in 1913, are delightful sketches that capture the idyllic nature of his native Norway and display a highly descriptive writing style, revealing the influence of Edvard Grieg. In 1941, Torjussen fled Norway to escape the Nazis. One of thirty-eight passengers on a ship that departed Volda on October 24, 1941, he arrived in Scotland three days later. Torjussen is best known for this tone poem, *To the Rising Sun.*

**Joc cu bâtă** (*Stick Dance,* from *Romanian Folk Dances,* Sz. 56), by Béla Bartók (1881-1945)
Bartók spent many years traveling, researching, and recording the folk melodies of every day, hardworking people in Turkey, Northern Africa, Yugoslavia, Bulgaria, Slovakia, and his native Hungary. His research and interest in folk music and rhythm became an essential aspect of his writing, and he created a unique musical vocabulary that is quintessentially his own. Listen to the Romanian rhythms and melodies in this folk dance and you will be transported to another time and place. This particular piece is about a dance with sticks or a game played with a stick, from Mezöszabad, a district of Maros-Torda, in Transylvania, Romania. It is merry and energetic with a cheerful, syncopated melody. Bartók is considered to be one of the most important composers of the 20th century.

**Golden Leaves** (from *Piano Album),* by Dimitar Ninov (1963-   )
Dimitar Ninov is a Bulgarian music theoretician, composer, and teacher. In Bulgaria he was conductor of a children's choir, and gave private lessons in harmony and *solfeggio* (the sol-fa singing technique). He also arranged songs and musicals. After earning degrees in music theory and composition from the State Academy of Music in Sofia, Bulgaria, he went on to earn a doctoral degree in composition from the University of Texas at Austin. His music often depicts vivid images, as in this piece about autumn leaves.

**On the Farm** (*Na farmě,* from *Fables,* H. 138), by Bohuslav Martinů (1890-1959)
The Czech composer Bohuslav Martinů was born in a small town on the Bohemian side of the Bohemian-Moravian border which is now the Czech Republic. His first studies were in the violin. After attending the Prague Conservatory, he became a teacher of the violin and began to compose. In 1923 he moved to Paris, France to study, and soon became a prolific composer, writing in every instrumental and vocal genre. He became one of the greatest Czech composers of his generation, and a major international figure known for his concertos and chamber music. *Fables,* composed in 1924, is one of his delightful solo piano pieces.

**Run, Run!** (from *Memories of Childhood*), by Octavio Pinto (1890-1950)
This Brazilian composer was trained as an architect, and studied piano. He married the Brazilian pianist Guiomar Novães, and they made their home in São Paulo. Pinto wrote a number of pieces for his internationally renowned wife, who in 1956 was awarded the

Order of Merit from the Brazilian government as a goodwill ambassador to the United States. He published a number of piano miniatures, among them *Scenas Infantis* and *Children's Festival.* His fellow Brazilian composer Heitor Villa-Lobos wrote a charming suite for the Pinto/Novães children.

**A Blown-Away Leaf** (from *On An Overgrown Path*), by Leoš Janáček (1854-1928)
Leoš Janáček was born in Moravia (now part of the Czech Republic) near the Polish border. He studied at the Prague Organ School, and became the conductor of the Czech Philharmonic, director of an organ school, and a professor of composition. He had a deep interest in folk melodies, collecting and arranging Moravian folk music as well as Moravian folk dances. Janáček's frequent letters to his friends chronicled his life in detail and serve as a "catalogue" of his compositions. *On An Overgrown Path* is a work consisting of fifteen miniatures he composed from 1900 to 1911. Janáček listened and wrote down the sounds of nature and people around him, and these melodic and rhythmic motives are important compositional techniques in his programmatic compositions. He is considered to be one of the finest composers of opera in the twentieth century.

**Busy Toccata** (from *Reaching Out, for Solo Piano*), by Emma Lou Diemer (1927-    )
Emma Lou Diemer began playing and composing piano music as a child, and by the age of thirteen became the organist at her church. Having majored in composition at Yale University and Eastman School of Music, she studied composition and piano in Brussels on a Fulbright scholarship, and later at Tanglewood. After receiving a doctorate from Eastman, she joined the faculty at the University of Maryland and later, became a professor at the University of California. She also served as composer-in-residence with the Santa Barbara Symphony. Her music, much of it commissioned, has been published and recorded.

**Moment sérieux** (*A Serious Moment,* from *Pour les Enfants, Vol. 4*),
by Alexandre Tansman (1897-1986)
Alexandre Tansman was a Polish-born French composer and pianist. He studied music at the Łódź Conservatory.  Although he won three prizes in the Polish National Music Competition, critics considered his style too bold. Tansman moved to Paris where he was quick to achieve international success. His music retained many distinctively Polish features, such as mazurka rhythms and Polish folk melodies. He also wrote collections of polonaises, nocturnes, impromptus, waltzes, and other Chopinesque miniatures. His many other significant works include vocal music for children.

**Petit Musique** (Opus 33, No. 8), by Florent Schmitt (1870-1958)
This French composer and pianist was born to music-loving parents in Lorraine, near the German border. He studied piano and harmony, and attended the Paris Conservatoire, studying with the influential and talented Gabriel Fauré. He developed close friendships with the French composers Maurice Ravel and Erik Satie, and frequented concerts of Russian music. He had an independent spirit, and was considered a musical pioneer. His compositions are admired for their energy and grandeur, and include chamber and keyboard music—preludes, rhapsodies, waltzes, easy pieces, suites, dances, pieces for four hands—as well as works for stage, orchestra, and voice.